CARDBOARD MAN

CARDBOARD MAN

BY

JOSHUA MYER

Brewer Publishing   Searcy, Arkansas   2025

PUBLISHED BY BREWER PUBLISHING

The colophon is a trademark of Brewer Publishing.

Library of Congress Cataloging-in-Publication Data
Myer, Joshua E.
Cardboard Man: poems / by Joshua Myer. – 1st ed.
p. 50 cm. 15.24x22.86
ISBN: 979-8-218-74470-0
2025944495
https://lccn.loc.gov/2025944495

Edited By Alec Brewer
Cover Art by Brewer Publishing

Manufactured in the United States of America
First Edition

For my country, my love.

Foreword

I'd like to thank Stacie, my dad, Ciro, and Alec; everyone who keeps encouraging me to write.

      In 2024, a publisher I edit for asked "have you been working on anything interesting?" I showed him the first half of this chapbook and asked what he thought. I had been obsessively watching the news, half convinced that, if I could just get the right words out, I might be able to somehow stop what I saw as the rise of fascism in American politics.

Cardboard Men

The cardboard man waves his pretense of arm;
when the laser breaks and the sensor trips,
he plays a recording of the universal greeting
"howdy partner, and welcome to --"

but before he can tell you the name of the store
you imagine an army of flattened marlboros,
men with flat cowboy hats, flat holsters,
flat pistols and flat boots. They march.

Flat Willy's red bandana flags down lost practices,
a robotic wall with a painted face, a signpost
messenger welcoming dry desert winds
with his tired motor in his tired arm.

We have a statue in Manhattan Bay,
that holds a torch defiant to the darkness
and welcomes the poor, tired and hungry
to a country, where they manufacture

cardboard men.

Cadillac, with a Shovel in the Trunk

They plant the iron scraps in the crucible,
and shovel the coal in the furnace. Turn the key.
They pump the gas and push the pedal.

Their hands are calloused
when they cruise the boulevard
they leave the dust and smoke behind them.
Paint it pink - a black tar striped with yellow
smoke pours from their pleather mouths,
pouches heavy with stones,
rusty saws and hammers.

Golden fields of wheat that yawn -
two oceans and a dream,
and a shovel in the trunk,
in case of emergencies.

Think about the things you might have to bury
every time you dig a hole.

The earth always asks for something
in return for every nugget
of a purple mountain.

The roads stretch forever
and they keep building new ones.
With mesh orange vests and hard hats,
they dig and scrape with their iron nails,
drive giant steel oxen and silver horses.

Flagpoles and Babies

Steel and concrete, cables, pulleys, and mills -- these raise the flag.
These command the salute that captures the praise of wild them.
The tall thin monolithic monument to the steel age,
carabiners clank, sway in the winds, bellowed from vast forges.

These regiments demand a human sacrifice
as strong, steady hands resist motion.

The wind still carries the destinies of wild -
them to die on distant shores.
Their blood will be spilled in foreign lands;
their dog tags may return.

The mechanist knows there is no liberty in motion. The earth tugs blood
and the wheel turns and the press squeezes out another combat knife
and the wheel turns to sharpen it's edge against a steady hand
and the wheel turns and raises the human flag of battle.

Will you shake from fear or excitement,
when the wheel chooses you,
to stand before your enemy
a distant abstract target?

Swerve Satisfaction or How to Miss a Point

Black, brown, pink, orange, red, and white skins -
all love freedom.
I don't know anyone with blue skin,
but blue skins probably love freedom too.

To be free we must:
shoot skeet, spit, chew, and fuck,
wear high heels and raise a family,
go naked through the fields of summer,
paint what we feel and damn the consequences.

We must go to the market,
and spend our collection of change.
We must chew our food and swallow,
believe that we can make friends,
and that change is possible.
That we can lose friends
and survive.

And when the songs on the radio end,
I'll raise my arms to the sky
to believe that I am free.

Give me the bass; let me feel us dance.
Give me the rhythm in my down-low bones.
Let's protest the flapping color of freedom:
red and white, but blue no longer?

Blue is the color of freedom, and we've missed the point.

The Spoke Says - Don't Tread on Me Either

A kitten's tail and a southerner agree
on subjects of mutual importance.
Most people don't know what it means
to live with just a slim chance,
to be married to the land without
the metal tools to shape it,
to long for a ring, a band or a hoop,
though you happen to know how to make it.

But the country is changing.
I'd wager we'll sell it all
to attend our square dances,
dine together in banquet halls,
speak with the voice of the peoples,
and hear a speech that heals
our collective emotional scars.

We find our churches searching for steeples;
we find our friends by breaking bread.
We find our beliefs by chasing sunsets;
we find our God when we bury the dead.

A kitten's face may bare its teeth,
and hiss when you surprise it,
but forget the offense in a New York minute,
when it searches for a teat,
or something to eat;
it will put the tail behind it.

The Boys in Blue

She wants to move away from the city
but she's worried about the color of skin
and she doesn't want someone telling her
what she can and can't do
when she knows ...

It doesn't help that every time
she gets five minutes to herself
some screaming kid demands.
It doesn't matter what it wants,
when she knows ...

And then the boys in blue show up,
asking politely if they may enter her house.
Their shields are brass encased in leather.
Clubs are made of carbon. Lightning guns,
teflon weave vests and hundreds of rounds of

black
powder
death.

The Right to The Starving Populus

Our rights are in danger of being misunderstood,
the right to remain silent has never done me good.

The right to vote exists, if you can prove citizenship,
the right to an attorney, if you can afford innocence.

The right of representatives to follow their money
is even sweeter and more sacred than wildflower honey.

The right to bear arms we may take to our graves
while nazis take pot shots at runaway slaves.

The right to assemble frightens good lawful kings -
political secrets are frightening things!

Dissidents among us may forever be meeting
as certainly as freedom is forever fleeting.

The right to truth has been laid between lines,
as the press remains free to maim and malign.

The right to a trial is often supposed
(in times of vague conflict, it may be deposed).

What other rights do we have left
retaining weight, utility and heft?

The right to forgive? The right to cry,
to pursue liberty or happiness, to lie?

My right is your right - our rights are the same,
please understand these are patriots' claims.

Right handed we wave as our rights parade past.
We all hunger for freedom, left alone as we fast,

paper ballots dancing as the nation accelerates/
becomes a free country of apolitical reprobates.

Song Without a Hero

Under the bridge there lives a troll,
on whom life extracts a heavy toll.
He cannot afford a fire to warm,
to protect himself from bodily harm.

I know a man who sleeps in the ground.
He snores but never makes a sound.
He knows a woman richer than gods;
she owns the land on which she trods.

We all know the law that shackles the wrist,
the prying bar and locking twist.
We all hear the siren's warning away
the brave and the wicked, night and day.

I didn't listen to what I was told
in the classroom where I grew so old.
But I can afford a roof made of clay,
to spend the days in this frivolous play.

New American Transcendentalists

We were the children who sat in rows studying freedom,
looking out the window or staring at the clock, wishing
time would suddenly stop, or else obey our young whims,
completing our problem sets according to the instructions.

We were another generation of dreamers, quietly chiseling
answers into our desks, questions recycled many times over.
Instead we read the light projected onto whitewash walls,
cinder block stacks and books in solid text. We were allowed

fifteen minute breaks twice a day, twenty three minutes for lunch.
When the bell rang, we were free to leave, receive our marks,
walk home through public parks. This was our week of five days,
underpaid teachers taught us how to think and what to say:

When your time comes, you will have to work to convince
everyone that you are worth the cost of your survivorship.
You will be at the mercy of the free market, anonymous surplus.
No one will care to read you the rules that you don't already know.

For the first time, you will be truly free to sell your time, to earn your food,
and understand the value of work. At last, you will be ready to share

our American dream.

Chains and Gangs and Cavateous Voids

Peoples are captive to loyalty or shame,
fears of violence and pain,
concrete walls and metal bars,
good jobs and familial bonds.

Someday, you may regret to find yourself
sucking the days through a sunbeam straw,
pieces of paper telling you to bend
and set your hands on the cold hard wall.

You promised you would pay your debts.
How everyone pays? With regrets.

Thieves do their business in the daytime:
go to the bank, the market or the gym.
The best thieves pay their bills carefully;
hands are like water, constantly flowing,
filling the cavateous void left behind
by the glacial progression of wealth
trailing dry and wrinkled valleys.

The Prison Industrial Shag

Feet on the floor,
toes on the line,
hands at your side and memorize
your spot on the ground and
close your eyes.

Every hour is a day,
every month is a year
and it's time for mandatory self improvement.

The sky is blue
and the grass is green
and when you get out of here
you won't have anything.

Poor, poor you, with nothing to do, and plenty of time to repent.
Gum scrapers, paper files, improper procedure and
yard time, hard time, ragtime, bagged time.

Paper weights, license plates,
rock breaking, back aching, soul shaking,
day making, leaf raking, pay-rate-change-lag time.
Chow time, how time? ragtime, shag time.

Community Chest

I don't know you and you don't know me;
you could be a member of this community,
approximately symmetrical humanoid that you are
but you just need to land on the right kind of square.

Then we will put you in a dank cramped room
so we can catch up on your correspondence.
When you are properly smoked in darkness,
you will need to reacclimate yourself to light.

Your initiation is a neighborhood barbeque,
complete with all the fixings - German potato salad,
brightly colored ketchup and American cheese,
buns from the bun factory, meat from the house,
and greens from the field. Thin sliced tomatoes.
Onions, oh onions! Each layer is another layer.

If you can make it there, you can make it anywhere
(get a job before you are delirious with hunger),
wash clean the stench of your mother's afterbirth.
Her chest was ample, but yours is damn near empty.

From Her Lips Erupted Factual Violence Against My Holy Nation

Two bowed and perfect hills have silhouetted a great ball of fire
spreading rays like fingers grasping the still earthen mounds
spewing forth from the ancient valley and tinting the sky orange;
she told me her proud existence
about rights so divine and how she likes to protest,

Politics is flush with faceless low-grade chopmeat pundits,
eager to climb the tiny mountaintop and preach down sermons
on you poor, unsuspecting, simple folk. They are ready to rain
hellfire and devastation from God's almighty fist of truth unto you
because they are so proud.

But beware! I am the one true burger king exiled from his home,
kept from his rightful throne. I will never bow to your floppy fries
nor will I yield to your entitled rants or your prideful cans and cants.
I declare vengeance on your mass marketing! I claim damages
for years of willfully ignorant wrongdoings against my face unseen.

My holy nation, my sacred home, my one true love,
Truth is coming for thee.

Don't Hate the Sinner

Sin is always original;
if it isn't original, it's not really sin.

So I bought an empty tube.
How will we get the toothpaste back in?

Where does your mind go when you are waiting?

The heavy number you can accept
before the deli counter. Corned beef.

It is your ticket to the show,
permission to enter
the promised land.

Cows also feel anxious
waiting for the slaughter:

Is it wrong to look forward?
Is it wrong to look back?

I try to not hate
what I don't understand.

But the ultimate resolution
isn't obvious -
either to Reuben or Rachel?

Advanced Raw Man

His green yard was pristinely sculpted long
before you climbed over his perfect picket fence and made
signs from the reclaimed lumber denouncing his right to preempt
with an automatic spray.
Now you must stand your ground

and

fear the homeowner.

Like a martyr, he will stretch out his open arms
as he stands straight and tall
singing America the Beautiful as loud as he can bare
until his patriotic throat is bleeding.

Communism is a joke. We kicked their ass
and we'll do it again and again until there are no
communists left to beat up.

Then, he'll buy us all a round
and complain about communists.

He won't put on a mask or take a shot. He won't slow down.
He is the final sentinel,
the penultimate patriot,
the last line in the sand
and he is multiplying

Open Letter to America

Forget what you know about Jesus and Muhammed.
Forget about Israel and abortions for a second.

Did the CIA evolve from eggs or dinosaurs?
Does Bigfoot know about the UFOs?
Who watches the watchers?
Who folds the clothes?

How many neighbors does it take
to screw in a lightbulb?
Is crime up or down?
What is under my dressing gown?

How many cars should we sell today?
How much company should I keep?
How many roads must a man walk down
before he can die in his sleep?

I sure am glad that I voted.
I think I'm going to think
about the chauvinists and the fascists,
and the abyssal electric sink.

I Voted

I want to wear my sticker all year round,
the participation trophy 18 years in the making.
I popped my cherry in the voting booth,
fucking everybody with my smile.

I dip my toes in the sand
the cigarette butts and broken needles
weedling their way into my personal space.
Paranoia.

I smile at the sunset.
I smile at the thunderhead and I smile at the breakers.
I grin with my eyes and their long eye shadows.
I grin at the tiny fiddlers burrowing.

It's popular to hate them,
eroding our concrete
barriers and foundations.
Also, Justin Bieber.

I wake up the next morning thinking:
I should have left my ballot empty.
It could be so stupendously easy
to just get my sticker.

Prose and Khans

I'm trying to figure out where I stand --
to the left or the right of Genghis Khan.

On the one hand, I'm firmly against placing heads on spits,
which attracts too many stray dogs (mongol mongrels) ...

But I can see the virtue of building walls from skulls,
at least as a temporary measure.
As long as a person is dead, they can't really find
a use for their skull anyway
and I certainly agree with his stances
on education and public works ...

But the real question is: how does the man feel
about abortion? I am certain he is pro-life.
Nevermind, how am I supposed to support
a candidate I can't share a meal with?
I'm sure we would have a lot to talk about:
when is a horse too old to eat?

Desperate times call for desperate measures,
so too, great deficits belie even greater inequities.
I'm firmly in favor of returning to a horse based military.

But what happens when we run out of enemies and find ourselves
stranded on the steppes of Asia with nothing but our bickering siblings
and a cold long winter of sore hips and weakening eyesight?

I'm Lovin It

I didn't always eat food fast but now
I like to sit in a McDonald's booth
watch people come in, use the bathroom, leave,
listen to the constant beeping of the broken
frier chanting a corporate mantra,
warding off evil -- om ... om ... om ...

Smell the fat of the sacred cow sizzling in the air
and the stinging ammonia of recently mopped floors.
I am alone with my paper bag, a toy
stuffed with the packaging from my meal,
thin skins drying in the halogen,
dissolving in the spray from the soda fountain,
my happy valley depleting a mountain of fries,
each one a bald fell pine in a haphazard pile.

The earth is banana yellow and cherry red.
My fingertips are dabbed with ketchup and my eyes
glaze cool as a frozen apple pie. I pray for the holy moment
and follow a salt breeze and the spent fry oil

away to a distant land;
perhaps, we will meet again
in the spice markets of India,
when (I too) shall devour the world.

The Blue Pill

It isn't medicine to any
known disease
but you take it and you take it
and you try try try
to play the field of
why oh why

defend a little patch of grass
your birthright guarantees
entitled to be buried
with your government cheese.

And you can be buried with the flag of your choice,
and you can cry fire in your digital voice
and you try try try
to leave a beautiful corpse.
Of course?
Of course, of course.

The Red Pill

Once upon a time, there was a Ronald Reagan
strong and kind, and kind of funny too.

There was fact and fiction and
periodicals to serve as reference,
libraries flush with unambiguous
joy and patriotism!

Oh how we waved! Like embers of grain we waved,
like tidal shoals we sloughed, like
barrels of crude we cracked
and split into the dividend
(our minds we wracked).

High, we hiked!
Our flags were homemade,
our shoes were cheaper;
phonecalls cost a dime, letters a nickel.
Back then, your word was worth something.

Once upon a time, there was a JFK,
the last personality of the television age.
Imagine: my brother and I, gone fishing out on the lake,
hooks dragging under the water, our lines pulled taught against
unseen forces chomping at the bit,
(shooting the breeze at the wall to see what might stick),
cans of beer keeping us cool as
Godzilla and King Kong come along
and knock us down again.
Bulls and bears and snapping snares,
and John F. Kennedy laughing along.

Once upon a time, there was Rambo-Charles Bronson/Steven Segall.
When his nose got bloody-knocked down he would pick himself up
and beat the crap out of the bad guy,
but, when it comes right down to it,
who can you trust? They all lie.
Remember the recounts?

This is no country for old men.

It's Felt

Touching his shirt you can taste the rain.
Shaking his hand you can feel the sweat.

This is the best
he can hope for.
Either kind will do.
A carnival for two.
All puffed up
his shoes in tatters;
imagine the paper
in his pockets ...

I'm sorry I couldn't do more.
It's beer and it's cold.
Happy Birthday.

I only have one thing left to fear,
but it's everywhere I turn to look.
When it rains, we get wet.
Don't mind so much.

My name is Joshua.
He said he was James
and asked me if I knew the meaning.

It is known
that when two people meet and discuss the law,
their meal has been blessed.
I carried home my heavy groceries.
I made a stir fry for dinner.
It tasted good, like salt.

MAGA

A patriot, a Jew and a Nazi walk into a bar.
Two out of three people are liars.
Don't trust false messiahs.
Politicians all are liars.

What did I do to be so black and so blue?
Two out of three ain't so bad.
I could do better in standup.
And then I wouldn't have to worry about the truth

It's a joke! It's a joke! Can't you read?
Ride the carousel. Mount the steed.
Women love me.
Fish fear me! I am

a dark shadow over a lake.
I am a drop in a bucket.
I am a man who remembers

yesterday's breakfast.

Survivors

If someone else can do a thing, so can you. It can always happen again.
She squeezed my hand to make sure I heard her. Listen. You can.

But her eyes said more than that. They won't come for you first,
but they will come for you. They will come for you. They will.

Starvation makes anyone weak, so never pass up a meal.
Try the pickled herring. A gun doesn't care who holds it.

Measure twice and cut once. Use a pencil not a pen.
Use the tools you have to make the tools you need.

I have more aphorisms than anyone will ever need.
What haunts me more is a question:

Where will I go?
Grandpa was a doct-or.

He used to say, "the most common things happen most commonly."
We're all sick and we only get sicker. Things fall apart.
It can happen again.

Dad was a lawyer.
Mother was a teller.
A survivor is a teacher.
A teacher is a friend.

the porter

ahem.

there is a spirit to every doorway
whether lintelless or cusped
beyond the edge of reservation.

for every room there is a doorway
and a spirit to usher you in
where a simple thankyou would suffice.

your luggage is taken for granted.
your luggage is carried by angels.
as your body is ferried on dollies.

your folly is henceforth a living thing
alive in your prison jungle-mind
a corridor for blood and questions

the dreamer

one and only
thoughts of you
like ripples on a pond
slip swiftly towards the surface

deep in this
palace dungeon
walls mean little
to the living ghosts of monarchs

furniture
brought from manifestos
all together in the mind realm
comfort the departed

bodiless
they pass the time
discussing enlightenment
reclining

the cobbler

the heel and the road are the same
and both are scraped together from trivium.

to a long-enough road our feet are disposable.
you grind the bones to dust and mix into a glue.

glue will hold together the skins
of so many callous animals,
for some time
stitches may reinforce
along the direction you intend to walk.

ankles grind and chafe
a pain that leads to resting,

but these are good roads and strong,
that lead to great cities. how could
evil grow where no weeds fit
between the hard smooth facets of creation?

the singer

outbreath and in,
bade the machine of her
and her mother also sang.

without a hand
hard wet sounds softly
from the mouth

tore a hole
into the reason.
i spilled out

the teller

the counting occurs within.

each unit of the rhythm marks
the thumbing
as by pages of a book
written within
and titled "the amount of".

everything is wrapped in paper,

especially wrinkles
on the face or on the hand
printed and bound in cloth.

we are bound
to proclaim our faith in numbers
beside the reckless train of history.

this polite exchange of names
will be cut

crossed with avenues of careful change
counted out by wrinkled hands
to a rhythm from within.

the heretic

the accuser whispers your denial
perched on the plastic pulpit
declares "these charges are false"
as absolute as your ephemeral guilt.

you feel a fraud
and wonder about the efficacy of abstinence,
how long you might last
in this tense arrangement

of two yoked horses,
otherwise strangers,
driving you to success
when all you wanted were groceries

the trusted

wherever i find freckles i am happy
to enumerate or connect by association
a constellation-generating-mythology.
stories for one, written on skin.

the young wanderer discovered
ever-warm water in a lowland spring.
this brought gold to the sky people
though every craftsman who drank

faced death. they became the trusted,
each marking their fate on their skin
melting their metal, shaping gods,
masks and stories. they inspired

a young explorer to draw a map
to connect artifact cities,
measure the trails walked diligently,
wandering in hope of a purpose.

that is a true covenant of love

the outdoorsman

they say, "wipe your feet" before you enter
the house
clean and stately
ripe seasoned furnitures
smooth like the walls of a deadfall
but not as solid an oak in its seventeenth winter

they ask, "where do you worship? Are you observant?"

a hawk might roam for miles
around its nest, parrots may follow
rolling seasons, robbins fattening
in the spring, pigeons picking trash-seed
from wheat like chickens in the farmer's yard.

Where does your mind go?

you are a leaf on a river of ants.

the cooper

Measure twice and cut once.
There's more sanding and shaving,
tugging and pressing
into the absence of the final craft
and this is shared-unburdened from hands:

planes sheared into tight fitting curves
a space ensconced by metal bonds
the vessel that will hold when full.
the vessel, simple, like a soul.

you see the cooper work with care
reflected in your worldly stare.

the neutrality of creation bared

the sapient

avoids the cementing eye lock
holds hands with angels
and they hardly speak

they hardly ever speak
and when they do it's too correct
and often to correct.

they want to build a machine
that can explain the differences
between the animals in the wheel-that-speaks

they want to make a picture
of the unwinding wax core
its rusty turning scrawl

all so you can speak and say

the treeman

you offer fruits so freely,
growing unselfishly, without self-burden.
i long to be this tree
with it's strong trunk.

man can be cut down so easily,
snapped and dragged back into the earth
as he trades paper for fruit
easily as leaf for wood

none may conquer
the treeman; his orchard grows wild,
sweat bubbles up like a spring.
he toils as you toil

with your plow in the dirt
your back bent crooked
as clouds like sheep's wool
tempt you skyward

the eggman

they are born in pairs:
the source and deception birthed instantaneously,

light and darkness first reaching into each other
from the same shallow egg

but we are born alone and frightened
like a shout into a paper bag

the eggman climbs the mountain,
sees the valley unaltered by wind, by time,
a land containing what is and what could be.
it is reality and all who play,
the loser and the winner
weirdly emulsified.

male and female without meaning
dissolve before the mighty egg:
a precession of the division of
a meaning of divine loneliness
devising the very definition of time
the finished completion of children
generating future heredity
a crude/cold percentage
cracked and fried.

its just an idea,
fertile in the valley,
nested by the void.

the idea is lonely/
but its twin lives deep
within the ideal mountaintop

the oilman

they lied to you. you are not
immune to the black coffee
being pumped into your body.

(cold welds covered in oil)

as he shakes your hand you lose
a tangible piece of the puzzle,
dilapidated business cards --

like a rasp tapping on your back
he whispers that
you dropped your wallet.

his mind is filled, a pit of tar
slowly churning out hits
his sticky club-like fingers
covered in your blood.

until the reptilian corpses of your parents
he devours.

desire! how he desires mastery
over all the woodlands creatures
as he bares his teeth from atop
the rigged platform

the gutter

they designed his arteries like spillways
out from his heart towards his liver
a soup of bilge and liquid suet
that keeps the salt high in his arms
so he can hook the bloated belly.

out from his heart and into his arms
the early morning liquor warms
and steadies the hand that grips the blade
that looses the stomach onto the floor
flowing like a river, searching for a moor.

two, three, four ... he easily loses count ...
the fountain splatter on his apron and sleeves ...
the cats that follow him home
and the name he is trying to remember ...

the rockman

i am unsure
beyond the jackal-headed raconteur
and a slave to ancient ways once led
by orpheus in his sleeping head.

the rockman smiles through his broken teeth
which offers an easy rung to reach,
the subject of greyed eyes,
the bluing abject wonder
spooned a secret jackpot prize.

we will form bonds that crumble,
play music ripe with thunder,
all in the grey of eyes ...

still the rockman hordes his treasure
like a salamander, slick with leisure
crawling back into a crevasse,
sinking into secret pleasure.

this i saw within the grey of eyes:

pieces taken from his faces,
by scavengers of outer spaces
left just enough for him to smile.

i breathed the smoke still in his lungs,
that smelt of porridge, earth and dung
and walked with him along a while

but his tight closed fist will never share,
secrets he will never bare

scream and let all beware:
a jackal-headed lover,
stones for eyes

the producers

as far as investments go
it's swollen, bloated and ugly.
You retain control, only of the principle,
waiting in the wings, deciding
who wears what and when,
doling out the payroll.

within them is a pink safe,
capable of constructing more safes,
an army of imperfect replicas
hiding their secret incalculable value -
torsos filled with torsos, busts
to be placed on pedestals,
erected for one fantastic purpose:
to be a spectacle.

life is a spectacle,
a charade for all involved,
the passive onlookers
and the witless actors
contorted in helix splendor.

Everything happens so much.